# *Christmas Gift*

To Betsy –
Happy Holidays
*[signature]*

Cover artwork & B&W illustrations p. 4, 24: Deborah Cidboy

Photograph of dog, p. 40: © Justin Fabian, 2006

ISBN-13: 978-0-9846347-6-7

ISBN-10: 0-9846347-6-2

Author's website: Yesterplace.com

Published by:

tm

ThomasMax Publishing
P.O. Box 250054
Atlanta, GA 30325
www.thomasmax.com

# *Christmas Gift*

# Susan Lindsley

ThomasMax

Your Publisher
For The 21st Century

## Acknowledgments

Many people have supported my efforts to assemble this book, especially my life partner Gail Cabisius.

Deborah Ann Cidboy deserves thanks for the wonderful art of the deer with funny feet—"Christmas Snow"—on the cover and for the artwork of the children missing Santa as they peek up the chimney.

Thanks to Justin Fabian for permission to include Sandy the dog in my labor of love.

Special thanks to Lee Clevenger for his support with this book—above and beyond the call of friendship.

*For Betsy*
*And all the other children of Dovedale*

# Table of Contents

# The Grocer

## A Christmas Story

The boy looked in the window filled with multicolored lights
Of reds and greens and yellows and of flashing blues and whites.

Tomorrow would be Christmas, but for him no Christmas cheer,
Just another morning, like the days of all the year.

Daddy dead and buried just a year ago September,
But hunger now was all he knew, and all he could remember.

Mama home and sick in bed, and Sister sickly too.
The boy began to quietly sob, not knowing what to do.

He wandered by the many stores, with food and gifts in piles,
Stores for just the wealthy stretching on and on for miles.

The grocer saw him reaching for the smallest pre-cooked ham,
And frightened him by saying, "Son, you'll need yourself a yam,

"And just a few more items for a Merry Christmas meal.
This is Christmas Eve, my son, you have no need to steal."

Quickly then he packed a box, too heavy for the boy,
Topping it with gifts to bring the children Christmas joy.

And so the grocer took the box and went home with the child
And, stepping in the dreary house, he felt his heart go wild.

For there was his Clarissa, whom another man had wed,
And since that day the grocer felt his heart and soul were dead.

And thus his act of Christmas love to bring another joy
Filled the grocer's stocking with a wife and girl and boy.

## A Deer with Funny Feet

Upon a crystal Christmas Eve, the stars were clear and bright
When a reindeer fawn was born, whose coat was snowy white.

Before the babe was on his feet, the reindeer gathered round
To say, "We'll never see this boy when snow is on the ground!"

When his mother named her son, she called him Christmas Snow
With hopes he'd change to reindeer brown as he began to grow.

Then someone said, "Oh! Would you look! This fawn has funny feet!
Every hoof has got three toes, and every toe a cleat!"

His mother licked her son with love, as if she didn't care,
And soon the fawn was bouncing 'round like any baby deer.

He joined with all the other fawns in learning how to fly,
But other reindeer shunned him, and they never told him why.

So working even harder, Snow was soon the very best,
And took the lead in every class on every reindeer test.

Still the others shunned him as the weeks and months went by,
So Snow went to his mother, and he asked her simply, "Why?"

"It's not because of funny feet or cause your hair is white,
But for always winning best of class in reindeer flight."

With the coming of the dawn, young Christmas Snow departed,
Missed by none but Mother, who was sad and broken hearted,

For mothers always miss a child who's somewhere far away,
But still she hoped her son would venture home again some day.

As the years went rolling by, he grew in pride and might,
Perfecting both his power and his skill in reindeer flight.

Pain and anger faded as a wisdom grew within,
And Snow could only shake his head at narrow-minded kin.

He told himself he was not wrong to do his very best,
For every one should always try to lead in every test.

He never turned to reindeer brown and did not choose his feet,
So why let others' jealousy become his own defeat?

Then one icy Christmas Eve, old Santa took a fall,
And sliding from a slippery roof came sleigh and deer and all.

The sleigh was quickly righted, but the deer said, in defeat,
"We can not stand on icy roofs without a football cleat."

Then Mother said, "Remember, now, my son of long ago,
The fawn that you called Funny Feet and I called Christmas Snow?

"I know that he can hold the sleigh in all this ice and sleet
Because each toe on every hoof has got a football cleat."

So they went to seek the one they all called "Funny Feet,"
But all they saw were miles and miles of snow and ice and sleet.

For in the land of sun and snow, the stag could not be seen,
Just his footprints in the snow would show where he had been.

Till Mother said, "He's yonder! And I know it without fail,
For I can see his footprints where he's walking on that trail."

And oh what tracks he left behind! They showed that all his feet
Had that extra toe that let him stand on ice and sleet.

In seconds they descended and they told of their defeat.
"Troubles make us wiser," said the stag with funny feet.

"Although my hide is different and I've got a funny hoof
I've finally learned to laugh at scorn—I'll hold you on the roof."

## Christmas Morning

Ice and winter everywhere,
Even crackling frozen air;
Squirrels huddled in the trees,
Snow instead of colored leaves.

A million diamonds in the frost,
A single snowflake bounced and tossed;
Mistletoe above the door,
Presents spilled across the floor.

Home fires burning clear and bright
With the coming of the night;
Children's laughter in the air,
Christmas morning everywhere.

## The Shepherd Boy

The night was deep and silent and the waxing moon was new;
The sheep paused in the silence on the hill as if they knew.

They crowded round the shepherd boy who only stared on high
In awe at all the glory of the star that lit the sky.

In silence more than silent and a stillness more than still
The music of the angels softly echoed from the hill.

The glory of the single star enlarged and grew more bright,
While music of the angels rose to fill the silent night.

He left his flock in silence on that winter night so mild
And, singing with the angels, went to see the Holy Child.

## Why Santa's Reindeer Fly

The snow is falling softly, bringing dreams of Christmas Day
And everywhere the children hope that Santa's on his way,
Riding in a sleigh they say can sail across the sky
Since that year that Santa taught his reindeer how to fly.

For long ago the reindeer simply ran along the ground
And went like magic lightning from the Pole the world around.
Then somewhere in our yesterdays the world was all agog
For Santa never reached a house—the deer fell in a bog;

Although the reindeer struggled, they spent Christmas Eve out there
Stuck within the muck and mire while children everywhere
Wept in disappointment at their stockings hanging bare,
Unsure if Santa just forgot or maybe did not care.

While in the bog that Christmas Eve old Santa heard them cry
And knew the time had come to teach his reindeer how to fly.

## Christmas Greetings

The smell of muffins in the air
And chimneys smoking everywhere,

Snow like icing on the trees
And frost that nips the morning breeze,

Children, eager for this day,
Wished their Christmas Eve away,

Everywhere, the sounds of greeting
Families and the neighbors meeting,

So I send you Christmas cheer
And wishes for a great new year.

## One Christmas Eve

Snow lay heavy on the streets and on the rooftops too,
And the climbing moon was turning snowy shadows blue

On the night I heard a voice, down on the street below,
"Merry Christmas to you all" and "Ho, ho, ho, ho, ho."

Looking from the window, all I saw was midnight snow
For shadows, blue and moving, filled the snowy street below.

Perhaps it's on the roof, I thought. It's Santa and his deer,
But who can tell at midnight if the roof is tracked or clear?

So when the morning came again, I walked the street below
And saw the tracks of reindeer and a sleigh across the snow,

And I saw the snow that lay so thick upon the roofs
Bore the marks of runners and of many reindeer hooves.

So tell me not that Santa's just an ancient children's tale
For I have heard his greetings and I've seen the reindeer trail.

## Christmas—98

Headlights cutting though the dark,
Snowflakes softly falling,
E-mail Christmas greetings now,
No more cards or calling.

No more toys for children now
No more clothes to wear,
Letters all to Santa say
"I only want software."

Christmas, cold with flurries,
And a lot of neon light,
But only Windows-98
Will make my Christmas bright.

## The Crystal Christmas

Although I'd heard his "Ho, ho, ho," I'd never seen St. Nick,
For whether we had rain or snow he came and went too quick
For me to see his deer or sleigh, much less the jolly man.
He seemed forever playing games of "Catch me, if you can."

But then last night a dreadful thing—the crystal ice was slick
Upon the roof, and down they slid: The deer, the sleigh, St. Nick.

I stood in awe and wonder at such a sight to see,
But all was quickly righted and Old Santa winked at me.

Then all the reindeer danced about as if to test their feet;
Old Santa said, "Then on we go," and quickly took his seat.

Without a sound they made a dash and swept into the sky;
They circled houses, then the town, and once more passed me by.

I watched them flying in the night until I could not see
The speck they were, and then I saw the gift he left for me.

For standing there upon the snow, a crystal deer so bright
I'll not forget ole Santa and the spill he took last night.

## A Vanishing Trail

I walked into the dawning while the world was still asleep,
Into the Christmas morning when the snow was lying deep.

The sunlight on the snowfall made a Christmas card of trees,
And far away I heard the sound of bells upon the breeze;

And then I heard a rooster crow, to call the world awake,
And turning, I saw hoofprints from the yard across the lake.

Beside the hoofprints ran a pair of tracks made by a sleigh
That headed west as if to keep ahead of coming day.

I followed out upon the lake, a mile from either shore,
Until the snow was smooth and I could see the tracks no more.

And what a puzzle then I faced, to try to figure where
The sleigh and deer could be, unless they rose into the air.

From in the west I heard a laugh, a jolly "Ho-Ho-Ho."
Then silence filled the morning, silence deep as Christmas snow.

## Unseen Images

Tinkling bells in darkness and the sound of hurried feet,
Children singing carols, moving shadows on the street.

Candles in the windows, giving night a golden glow,
Sweethearts stealing kisses underneath the mistletoe.

Every child now sleeping with a special Christmas dream—
Scooters or Monopoly or a pony gold and cream.

In a lonely shelter sleep a child and battered wife
Hoping that the ending year is not the end of life.

Before you open all your gifts underneath the tree
Reach, and help another, for she could be you or me.

## Christmas

Hurry, hurry,
People scurry,
Christmas Eve is nigh.

Taillights flashing,
People dashing,
One more gift to buy.

Sleigh bells ringing,
People singing,
Christmas in the air.

Snowflakes falling,
People calling,
Magic everywhere.

Presents shaking,
People baking,
Children filled with cheer.

Wreaths of holly,
People jolly,
Dreams of yesteryear.

## Merry Christmas

The snow lay like a carpet and the moon was riding high
When somewhere in the shadows of the night we heard his cry.

The "Merry Christmas" that we heard, so loud and crystal clear,
Let us know without a doubt that Santa Claus was near.

We all ran to the windows, sure that we would see St. Nick
Unless the jolly man had pulled a disappearing trick.

We saw just flowing moonlight, not a sleigh or deer at all,
And then we felt the shaking of his laughter fill the hall.

We hurried to our stockings, hoping Santa we would spy,
But he had come and gone and called "Goodnight" from in the sky.

So when the snow at Christmas turns the midnight shadows blue,
Listen for his greetings for you know the legend's true.

## Going Home

Snowflakes in December air,
Songs of Christmas everywhere;

Holly wreaths on all the doors,
Presents every child explores;

Snow men marching on the grass,
Bells that ring out midnight mass;

Windows glowing soft with light,
Call us home on Christmas night.

## Christmas Eve

Taillights, garlands for the roads,
The decorated trees,
The smell of cooking everywhere,
And laughter on the breeze,

Snow in boxes, snow in rolls,
Snow in all our dreams,
And presents filled with mystery
Are everywhere, it seems.

The sound of sleigh bells in our hearts,
And Christmas in the air,
Our resurrected childhood dreams,
And joy beyond compare.

## Christmas across the Tracks

The laughter of the children floated on the Christmas air,
Mingling with the smell of roasting turkey everywhere.

But down across the river in a tiny one-room shack
Heated by the coal the mother picked up on the track

Where the Norfolk-Southern ran a train of coal a day
And piled it extra high so some would fall along the way,

The mother with a baby girl just barely three years old
Wanted but a blanket so her baby wasn't cold.

And it never crossed her mind to think in terms of toys
But of shoes and jackets for the ever-growing boys.

When the children finally asked that Santa visit there
Other children told them that they never had a prayer

Of having Christmas turkey, or a toy, or anything—
And all the mother had to give was music she could sing.

But on that Christmas morning while she sang to bring them cheer
Noises from the outside grew both louder and more near—

Sounds of sleigh bells ringing and a hearty laughter too,
So to the door the mother and the children quickly flew.

And there across the yard lay all the mother's fondest dreams,
Blankets and some shoes and coats in matching color schemes,

Stockings filled with puzzles and with games and other toys
And a turkey labeled, "Love to Mama, from your boys."

## Musical Christmas

I heard the churches ring their bells so many years ago
On a Christmas morning when the world was white with snow.

And on a Christmas morning I saw horses stepping high
Making sleigh bells jingle as the team went clomping by.

Many are the songs I heard the Christmas singers singing
To the music of the bells that they themselves were ringing.

But now the only bells I hear upon the Christmas air
Float from new computer games in households everywhere.

## Twenty-First Century Holidays

The holidays are coming for the leaves have turned to gold,
And pumpkins from the garden patch have finally all been sold.

The crops have all been gathered and the hay is in the dry,
And we have finished planting all the autumn wheat and rye.

The holidays are coming; I've a million things to do,
Forty-seven gifts to buy, and all that baking too.

Gifts to buy while knowing all the colors may be wrong,
Sweaters that will never fit, and trousers far too long.

Cookies for the office keep me baking half the night
When I have a growing stack of Christmas cards to write.

The holidays are coming, with a million things to do.
And Oh! Will I be glad to see December finally through.

## Yesterday's Christmas

Mistletoe, and memories of the Christmases gone by
When the season meant we had pecan and apple pie.

Days when Dad could make the fire burn brilliant green and blue,
And we shipped out fresh pecans to everyone we knew.

Days when we recycled all the ribbons that we could,
And made our decorations out of paper and of wood.

Days of fun and laughter, and of Santa, fat and jolly,
When we never thought of buying mistletoe or holly.

Days when all the cattle got an extra bale of hay,
For cattle gave their manger on the distant Christmas day.

## A Father's Christmas

The wind is soft, the snow is deep, the sun and clouds are mixing,
And in the air the scent of goose and other Christmas fixings
Swirl into the laughter of the children in the snow
Making angels on the hills and snowmen down below,

Sliding down the hill with Dad, upon the Christmas sled,
Tumbling with the puppy with the perfect name of "Red,"
Setting up a barricade with lifting battle cry,
Dancing all about to dodge the snowballs flying by,

Going, shivering, back inside, dripping melting snow,
Heedless of the river flowing everywhere they go;

Christmas time, and Mother has to cook and clean and pray
While Father sleeps beside the fire or goes outside to play.

## Too Much Christmas

The children whooped and yelled at dawn, and shouted out their glee
And hurried with excitement to the gifts beneath the tree.

They opened gifts and opened gifts, and then they opened more,
Until the gifts and wrapping tangled all across the floor.

Abundance not remembered at the closing of the day
For satiated children can't remember what to play.

**ALSO FROM THOMASMAX PUBLISHING BY SUSAN LINDSLEY**

## BLUE JEANS AND PANTALOONS IN YESTERPLACE, $16.00

*Yesterplace* inhabitants included Flannery O'Connor, Susan Myrick of Gone With The Wind, cattle rustlers, shady politicians, world-renown scientists, murderers and a conjure woman. With neither television nor telephone, Susan and her sisters made up their games and songs, rode horses to the picture show, and played at Roy Rogers and Jesse James. Yesterplace transports readers into a rural community that most of us never knew and those who did have forgotten. From bootleggers to society leaders, she creates real people. Her writing echoes the sounds of possum hunts and trace chains, the smells of hayfields, magnolias and manure, and the beauty and sadness of country life.

*Yesterplace* won the Josephine Mellichamp Award for nonfiction from the Southeastern Writers Conference. "A must read for O'Connor fans" says William Monroe, Professor and Dean, the Honors College, University of Houston. Available for Kindle or Nook for $5.99.

**ALSO FROM THOMASMAX PUBLISHING**
**EDITED BY SUSAN LINDSLEY**

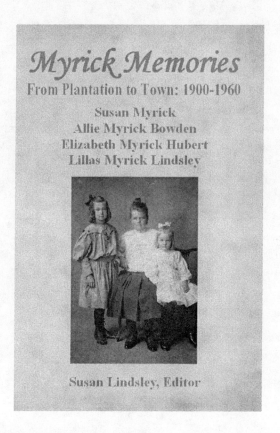

**MYRICK MEMORIES FROM PLANTATION TO TOWN: 1900-1960**

**$10.00**

Learn about race relations, including interracial marriages, in the early 1900s. Explore courtrooms and visit an old-fashioned prom. Learn about housekeeping and child care in the late 1800s. Read Susan Myrick's only published short story. Available for Kindle or Nook for $5.99.

"Susan Lindsley has recaptured a bygone era in *Myrick Memories*. The reader will enjoy getting to know about a time—a place—a family with a far-reaching legacy." -- **Del Ward, Host/Producer, WMAZ-TV, Macon, Georgia**

## ALSO FROM THOMASMAX PUBLISHING BY SUSAN LINDSLEY

## SUSAN MYRICK OF GONE WITH THE WIND:
## AN AUTOBIOGRAPHICAL BIOGRAPHY, $29.95

This book reveals the Susan Myrick that she hid from the world and recorded only in her diary. You will feel her anguish at the loss of love. You will feel her own fear at the prospect of having to face down David Selznick over the realities of the South's customs, agriculture, and other matters. You will also get a look into the private letters she wrote Peggy Mitchell, and learn about her ever-changing opinions of Hollywood personalities. . . and learn about the behind the scenes activities on the GWTW set. Available for Kindle for $9.99.

All ThomasMax books by Susan Lindsley, including additional copies of this book, are available through most bookstores and internet sellers. You may also purchase autographed copies of the books, subject to availability, directly from the author at the prices listed here. Contact Susan Lindsley at yesterplace@earthlink.net for ordering information.

# NOW AVAILABLE!

## SUSAN MYRICK ON DVD

From a TV interview

Sue discusses Peggy Mitchell

And

Making of *Gone With The Wind*

$10.00 + $3.00 S&H

From

Susan Lindsley

P.O. Box 33536

Decatur, GA 30033

OR

The Marietta Gone With The Wind Museum

## O YESTERPLACE AND OTHER POEMS

Return to your yesterplaces, to the times of banjos at dusk, to Roy Rogers and Trigger, to the chapel down the lane, and other childhood memories. Here's the title poem:

### O YESTERPLACE

O yesterplace, O yesterplace, my heart is there once more,
Dancing with the daffodils along the shadowed shore,

Walking in my yesterplace where music filled the air,
Banjos strumming in the night and laughter everywhere,

Rainbows in the summer sky and hayfields smelling sweet,
Ringing sound of horseshoes when we gallop down the street,

Crowing roosters in the dawn and hunting hounds at night,
Winter warmth beside the fire and kerosene for light,

Morning smell of biscuits and on Sunday, chicken frying,
Whippoorwills that fill the night with lonely, mournful crying,

Ghostly sound of childhood fears—a rustling in the wind,
O yesterplace, O yesterplace,
My heart is there in yesterplace and calls me home again.

**$12.00 + $3.00 S & H**

**From**
**Susan Lindsley**
**P.O. Box 33536**
**Decatur, GA 30033**

CPSIA information can be obtained at www.ICGtesting.com
Printed in the USA
LVOW060251171011

250764LV00002BA/9/P